INSECTS UP CLOSE

Milkweed Bugs

by Patrick Perish

BLASTOFF! READERS

BELLWETHER MEDIA • MINNEAPOLIS, MN

Note to Librarians, Teachers, and Parents:

Blastoff! Readers are carefully developed by literacy experts and combine standards-based content with developmentally appropriate text.

Level 1 provides the most support through repetition of high-frequency words, light text, predictable sentence patterns, and strong visual support.

Level 2 offers early readers a bit more challenge through varied simple sentences, increased text load, and less repetition of high-frequency words.

Level 3 advances early-fluent readers toward fluency through increased text and concept load, less reliance on visuals, longer sentences, and more literary language.

Level 4 builds reading stamina by providing more text per page, increased use of punctuation, greater variation in sentence patterns, and increasingly challenging vocabulary.

Level 5 encourages children to move from "learning to read" to "reading to learn" by providing even more text, varied writing styles, and less familiar topics.

Whichever book is right for your reader, Blastoff! Readers are the perfect books to build confidence and encourage a love of reading that will last a lifetime!

This edition first published in 2018 by Bellwether Media, Inc.

No part of this publication may be reproduced in whole or in part without written permission of the publisher. For information regarding permission, write to Bellwether Media, Inc., Attention: Permissions Department, 5357 Penn Avenue South, Minneapolis, MN 55419.

Library of Congress Cataloging-in-Publication Data

Names: Perish, Patrick, author.
Title: Milkweed Bugs / by Patrick Perish.
Description: Minneapolis, MN : Bellwether Media, Inc., 2018. | Series: Blastoff! Readers. Insects Up Close | Audience: Age 5-8. | Audience: K to Grade 3. | Includes bibliographical references and index.
Identifiers: LCCN 2017028749 | ISBN 9781626177161 (hardcover : alk. paper) | ISBN 9781681034096 (ebook)
Subjects: LCSH: Large milkweed bug-Juvenile literature. | Milkweeds-Juvenile literature.
Classification: LCC QL523.L9 P47 2018 | DDC 583/.956-dc23
LC record available at https://lccn.loc.gov/2017028749

Editor: Nathan Sommer   Designer: Steve Porter

Printed in the United States of America, North Mankato, MN.

Table of Contents

What Are Milkweed Bugs?   4

Life on the Plant   10

From Egg to Adult!   16

Glossary   22

To Learn More   23

Index   24

What Are Milkweed Bugs?

Milkweed bugs are common garden insects. Their black and orange colors stand out!

ACTUAL SIZE:

large milkweed bug

5

Milkweed bugs taste really bad. Their bright colors warn enemies to stay away.

Milkweed bugs have two long **antennae**. Their mouths are pointy and straw-like.

antennae

mouth

Life on the Plant

Milkweed bugs live near milkweed plants. These plants grow in fields and woods.

milkweed
plant

Milkweed bugs love to eat milkweed seeds. They also suck up plant **sap**.

FAVORITE FOOD:

milkweed
seeds

Some milkweed bugs **migrate** each fall. They travel south where winters are warm.

From Egg to Adult!

Female milkweed
bugs lay about
30 eggs a day. The
eggs **hatch** quickly!

eggs

Young milkweed bugs are called **nymphs**. They eat a lot!

MILKWEED BUG LIFE SPAN:
about 1-2 months

nymphs

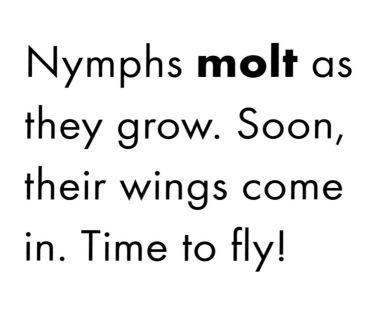

Nymphs **molt** as they grow. Soon, their wings come in. Time to fly!

wings

molt

Glossary

antennae

feelers connected to the head that sense information around them

molt

to shed skin for growth

hatch

to break out of an egg

nymphs

young insects; nymphs look like small adults without full wings.

migrate

to travel from one place to another, often with the seasons

sap

watery juices from a plant

To Learn More

AT THE LIBRARY

Hughes, Catherine. *Little Kids First Big Book of Bugs.* Washington, D.C.: National Geographic Society, 2014.

Moser, Lisa. *Stories from Bug Garden.* Somerville, Mass.: Candlewick Press, 2016.

Rustad, Martha E. H. *Milkweed Bugs.* Mankato, Minn.: Capstone Press, 2009.

ON THE WEB

Learning more about milkweed bugs is as easy as 1, 2, 3.

1. Go to www.factsurfer.com.

2. Enter "milkweed bugs" into the search box.

3. Click the "Surf" button and you will see a list of related web sites.

With factsurfer.com, finding more information is just a click away.

Index

antennae, 8, 9

colors, 4, 6

eggs, 16, 17

enemies, 6

fall, 14

females, 16

fields, 10

fly, 20

food, 13

garden, 4

hatch, 16

life span, 19

migrate, 14

milkweed plants, 10, 11

molt, 20, 21

mouths, 8, 9

nymphs, 18, 19, 20

sap, 12

seeds, 12, 13

size, 5

taste, 6

wings, 20, 21

winters, 14

woods, 10